SPORTS CARDS
Collecting, Trading, and Playing

Margo McLoone & Alice Siegel

SPORTS CARDS

☆ Collecting, Trading, and Playing

Foreword by PETE ROSE
illustrated with photographs

Random House/New York

Cover illustration/Richard Newton

Library of Congress Catalog Card Number: 79-64559
ISBN: 0-394-62020-8
This edition published by arrangement with Holt, Rinehart and Winston.

Manufactured in the United States of America
9 8 7 6 5 4 3 2 1
Random House Student Book Program Edition: First Printing September 1979

Special thanks to: Sy Berger, whose help and advice made this book possible; Pete Rose, a living legend and our dear friend; and to our editor Miriam Chaikin, who has proved to be inspirational and supportive in a very special way.

Additional thanks to Gloria Abramson, Marty Appel, Joe Garagiola, Jr., Norman Liss, Steve Schwartz, George E. Siegel, John Vergara, and Bob Weiss.

Photographs for Chapter 8, Making Things with Sports Cards, by Bob Weiss.

To Doug, John, George, Andrew,
Howard and Jimmy . . .
to their loving enthusiasm
and special help.

Contents

Foreword

The first time anybody ever showed me a Pete Rose baseball card was one of the proudest days in my life. I was just a rookie in the major leagues, and everything was a new experience; but few things seemed as important to me at the time. I knew I had arrived.

Most big league players spent more time playing than collecting during the growing up years, but everyone was aware of sports cards, and I learned a great deal about the major leagues from them. When I thought of playing in the majors, I thought of having my face on a card. It was one and the same.

My children are old enough now to enjoy collecting cards, and I hope it brings them the same satisfaction that I got when I was their age. We enjoyed learning more about this hobby by reading this book, and I'm sure you'll enjoy it too.

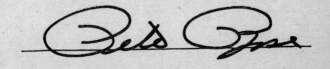

Schlei, New York National League
Early Tobacco Card

C. M. Daniels, Swimmer
Mecca Tobacco Company Card

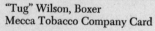

"Tug" Wilson, Boxer
Mecca Tobacco Company Card

W. J. Keating, Sprinter
Mecca Tobacco Company Card

D. B. Pratt, Second Baseman,
Boston American League
Early Caramel Candy Card

1

The Story of Sports Cards from Tobacco to Bubble Gum

The story of sports cards began in the 1880s when tobacco companies began to package cigarettes. They put small, colored picture-cards in the package. This was done for two reasons. One was to stiffen the package to keep the cigarettes from breaking. The other was to sell more cigarettes. The cards pictured many different athletes, such as horseback riders, boxers, billiard players, runners, swimmers, and baseball players. These were the first sports cards.

These sports cards became so popular and were so helpful in selling tobacco that soon candy companies began to give away cards with their products. The cards were used as a backing for caramel candies. These cards were larger than the tobacco sports cards and looked something like the bubble gum cards of today.

Believe it or not, bubble gum didn't appear until 1928. The

gum companies also hoped to sell more gum by putting a sports card in the package. This was the beginning of the combination of baseball and bubble gum.

World War II put a temporary stop to the making of bubble gum and sports cards. The government needed the paper used in the cards and the rubber used in gum for making war materials. Bubble gum and cards were not made again until 1948, after the war had ended.

In 1951, Topps Chewing Gum Company, the company that issues most of the cards that are available today, began to print

Eddie Joost, Shortstop,
Philadelphia Athletics
One of first cards made
after WWII, 1948, Bowman Company

Bob Feller, Pitcher, Cleveland
Indians, 1951, Topps Company

cards. They were designed so that a baseball card game could be played with them. Besides the athlete's picture, each card had strike, ball, hit, or out printed on it.

In 1952, Topps gave sports cards a new look. On the back of the card was printed information about the player, including his personal history, his playing statistics, and his team emblem. In addition, each card was given a series number, and for the first time, sports cards were issued in complete series. There is very little difference between these 1952 cards and the ones that you buy today.

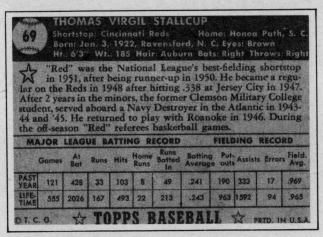

Virgil Stallcup, Shortstop, Cincinnati Reds
1952, Topps Company

2

Collecting Sports Cards

Sports have always been an important part of American life. Collecting sports cards is part of this tradition. You can get a sense of sports history and a feeling for the past when you collect cards. This is a popular hobby because it's both fun and easy to collect cards. Many enjoyable hours can be spent with sports cards—either by yourself or with friends. You don't have to spend a lot of money to collect cards, and it is possible to obtain some cards free. It is easy to keep and store your cards. Whether your collection is large or small, it won't take up a lot of space. An added bonus of sports card collecting is that you will have a chance to meet people and make new friends as you acquire more cards.

HOW TO COLLECT SPORTS CARDS
You will find it easy to collect sports cards because they are so readily available. If you have a small collection that you

want to add to, or if you are beginning to collect, you will find the following suggestions helpful.

Where to Buy Sports Cards

Most people begin their collections by buying cards. The usual way to buy them is in packages alone or with gum. These cards are sold in many places including supermarkets, candy stores, and five- and ten-cent stores. Since sports cards are issued seasonally, you will usually find baseball cards in the stores in the spring and summer, football cards in the early fall and winter, and so on.

One way to get many cards, without spending a lot of money, is to buy them at garage sales and flea markets. They are usually sold in large numbers. You may not be able to see all the cards when you buy them this way, but you can have fun sorting them out when you get home. There is a good chance you will find many cards for your collection in the bunch, and there are lots of things you can do with extra cards.

If you have a very strong interest in collecting and want to find particular cards, conventions and shows are good places to buy cards. You can also buy, sell, or trade cards by advertising in any of the sports card collectors' magazines listed on page 57.

Sports Cards for Free

There are some ways for you to get sports cards free. Your own energy and enthusiasm can be just as good as money. Start by looking in your own home. Look in out-of-the-way places, like the attic or basement or garage. You would be surprised at the number of people who have found forgotten boxes of old sports cards in this way. Ask your neighbors, friends, and relatives if they have sports cards they don't want to keep. Put up signs on public bulletin boards asking if anyone has cards they no longer want. Ask your friends to come to your home, with their cards, in order to play with them or trade them. This is a good way to get particular cards that you want in exchange for the extras you don't want. Also, watch the products your family brings home from the supermarket. You will find free cards in boxes of cereal, loaves of bread, and other foods. These are called premium cards.

KINDS OF COLLECTIONS
Series

A series is a complete set of cards issued in a year by a company. In order to collect a complete series you must find out how many cards are in the series. You can do this by getting a checklist. A checklist is a sports card which lists the names of all of the players appearing in that year's series. These checklists are found in packages among the regular sports cards. There are also books which have checklists. One of these is *The Sports Collectors Bible* and the other is *Sports Americana*. If you do not have a checklist, you can compare and exchange with your friends and learn which cards you need.

These cards are all numbered. Four separate series are issued each year, one series for each of the four major American sports: baseball, football, basketball, and hockey.

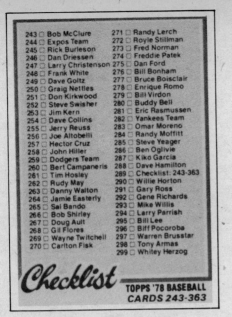

243 ☐ Bob McClure	271 ☐ Randy Lerch
244 ☐ Expos Team	272 ☐ Royle Stillman
245 ☐ Rick Burleson	273 ☐ Fred Norman
246 ☐ Dan Driessen	274 ☐ Freddie Patek
247 ☐ Larry Christenson	275 ☐ Dan Ford
248 ☐ Frank White	276 ☐ Bill Bonham
249 ☐ Dave Goltz	277 ☐ Bruce Boisclair
250 ☐ Graig Nettles	278 ☐ Enrique Romo
251 ☐ Don Kirkwood	279 ☐ Bill Virdon
252 ☐ Steve Swisher	280 ☐ Buddy Bell
253 ☐ Jim Kern	281 ☐ Eric Rasmussen
254 ☐ Dave Collins	282 ☐ Yankees Team
255 ☐ Jerry Reuss	283 ☐ Omar Moreno
256 ☐ Joe Altobelli	284 ☐ Randy Moffitt
257 ☐ Hector Cruz	285 ☐ Steve Yeager
258 ☐ John Hiller	286 ☐ Ben Oglivie
259 ☐ Dodgers Team	287 ☐ Kiko Garcia
260 ☐ Bert Campaneris	288 ☐ Dave Hamilton
261 ☐ Tim Hosley	289 ☐ Checklist: 243-363
262 ☐ Rudy May	290 ☐ Willie Horton
263 ☐ Danny Walton	291 ☐ Gary Ross
264 ☐ Jamie Easterly	292 ☐ Gene Richards
265 ☐ Sal Bando	293 ☐ Mike Willis
266 ☐ Bob Shirley	294 ☐ Larry Parrish
267 ☐ Doug Ault	295 ☐ Bill Lee
268 ☐ Gil Flores	296 ☐ Biff Pocoroba
269 ☐ Wayne Twitchell	297 ☐ Warren Brusstar
270 ☐ Carlton Fisk	298 ☐ Tony Armas
	299 ☐ Whitey Herzog

Checklist

TOPPS '78 BASEBALL
CARDS 243-363

Baseball Player Checklist
Topps Company

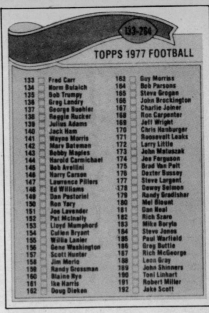

133-264

TOPPS 1977 FOOTBALL

133 ☐ Fred Carr	163 ☐ Guy Morriss
134 ☐ Norm Bulaich	164 ☐ Bob Parsons
135 ☐ Bob Trumpy	165 ☐ Steve Grogan
136 ☐ Greg Landry	166 ☐ John Brockington
137 ☐ George Buehler	167 ☐ Charlie Joiner
138 ☐ Reggie Rucker	168 ☐ Ron Carpenter
139 ☐ Julius Adams	169 ☐ Jeff Wright
140 ☐ Jack Ham	170 ☐ Chris Hanburger
141 ☐ Wayne Morris	171 ☐ Roosevelt Leaks
142 ☐ Marv Bateman	172 ☐ Larry Little
143 ☐ Bobby Maples	173 ☐ John Matuszak
144 ☐ Harold Carmichael	174 ☐ Joe Ferguson
145 ☐ Bob Avellini	175 ☐ Brad Van Pelt
146 ☐ Harry Carson	176 ☐ Dexter Bussey
147 ☐ Lawrence Pillers	177 ☐ Steve Largent
148 ☐ Ed Williams	178 ☐ Dewey Selmon
149 ☐ Dan Pastorini	179 ☐ Randy Gradishar
150 ☐ Ron Yary	180 ☐ Mel Blount
151 ☐ Joe Lavender	181 ☐ Don Neal
152 ☐ Pat McInally	182 ☐ Rich Szaro
153 ☐ Lloyd Mumphord	183 ☐ Mike Boryla
154 ☐ Cullen Bryant	184 ☐ Steve Jones
155 ☐ Willie Lanier	185 ☐ Paul Warfield
156 ☐ Gene Washington	186 ☐ Greg Buttle
157 ☐ Scott Hunter	187 ☐ Rich McGeorge
158 ☐ Jim Merlo	188 ☐ Leon Gray
159 ☐ Randy Grossman	189 ☐ John Shinners
160 ☐ Blaine Nye	190 ☐ Toni Linhart
161 ☐ Ike Harris	191 ☐ Robert Miller
162 ☐ Doug Dieken	192 ☐ Jake Scott

Football Player Checklist
Topps Company

BASKETBALL CHECKLIST 1-110

1 Scor. Avg. Ldrs.	27 Jim McMillian
2 F.G. Pct. Leaders	28 Matt Guokas
3 Free Throw Ldrs.	29 Fred Foster
4 Rebounds Ldrs.	30 Bob Lanier
5 Assists Leaders	31 Jimmy Walker
6 Steals Leaders	32 Cliff Meely
7 Tom Van Arsdale	33 Butch Beard
8 Paul Silas	34 Cazzie Russell
9 Jerry Sloan	35 Jon McGlocklin
10 Bob McAdoo	36 Bernie Fryer
11 Dwight Davis	37 Bill Bradley
12 John Mengelt	38 Fred Carter
13 George Johnson	39 Dennis Awtrey
14 Ed Ratleff	40 Sidney Wicks
15 Nate Archibald	41 Fred Brown
16 Elmore Smith	42 Rowland Garrett
17 Bob Dandridge	43 Herm Gilliam
18 Louie Nelson	44 Don Nelson
19 Neal Walk	45 E. DiGregorio
20 Billy Cunningham	46 Jim Brewer
21 Gary Melchionni	47 Chris Ford
22 Barry Clemens	48 N. Weatherspoon
23 Jimmy Jones	49 Zaid Abdul-Aziz
24 Tom Burleson	50 Keith Wilkes
25 Lou Hudson	51 Ollie Johnson
26 Henry Finkel	52 Lucius Allen

Basketball Player Checklist
Topps Company

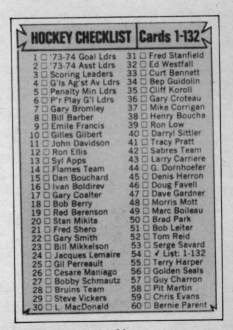

HOCKEY CHECKLIST Cards 1-132

1 ☐ '73-74 Goal Ldrs	31 ☐ Fred Stanfield
2 ☐ '73-74 Asst Ldrs	32 ☐ Ed Westfall
3 ☐ Scoring Leaders	33 ☐ Curt Bennett
4 ☐ G'ls Ag'st Av Ldrs	34 ☐ Bep Guidolin
5 ☐ Penalty Min Ldrs	35 ☐ Cliff Koroll
6 ☐ P'r Play G'l Ldrs	36 ☐ Gary Croteau
7 ☐ Gary Bromley	37 ☐ Mike Corrigan
8 ☐ Bill Barber	38 ☐ Henry Boucha
9 ☐ Emile Francis	39 ☐ Ron Low
10 ☐ Gilles Gilbert	40 ☐ Darryl Sittler
11 ☐ John Davidson	41 ☐ Tracy Pratt
12 ☐ Ron Ellis	42 ☐ Sabres Team
13 ☐ Syl Apps	43 ☐ Larry Carriere
14 ☐ Flames Team	44 ☐ G. Dornhoefer
15 ☐ Dan Bouchard	45 ☐ Denis Herron
16 ☐ Ivan Boldirev	46 ☐ Doug Favell
17 ☐ Gary Coalter	47 ☐ Dave Gardner
18 ☐ Bob Berry	48 ☐ Morris Mott
19 ☐ Red Berenson	49 ☐ Marc Boileau
20 ☐ Stan Mikita	50 ☐ Brad Park
21 ☐ Fred Shero	51 ☐ Bob Leiter
22 ☐ Gary Smith	52 ☐ Tom Reid
23 ☐ Bill Mikkelson	53 ☐ Serge Savard
24 ☐ Jacques Lemaire	54 ☐ ✓ List: 1-132
25 ☐ Gil Perreault	55 ☐ Terry Harper
26 ☐ Cesare Maniago	56 ☐ Golden Seals
27 ☐ Bobby Schmautz	57 ☐ Guy Charron
28 ☐ Bruins Team	58 ☐ Pit Martin
29 ☐ Steve Vickers	59 ☐ Chris Evans
30 ☐ L. MacDonald	60 ☐ Bernie Parent

Hockey Player Checklist
Topps Company

Teams

If you want to collect by teams, you must collect every player on a team for a year. In order to find out what cards are issued for any team, you can use a team-card checklist if issued. This team-card checklist is a sports card with the names of the players on the team for that year. These checklists are found

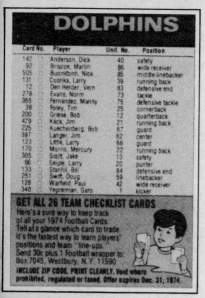

Miami Dolphin Football Team Checklist, Topps Company

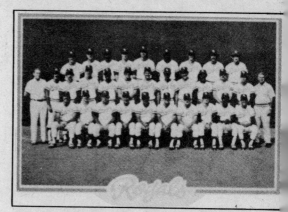

Royals Baseball Team Checklist, Topps Company

Players listed on a team card.

20

in packages along with the regular sports cards. If you don't have a checklist you can compare and exchange your cards with friends to learn which ones you need.

Specials

The companies that issue sports cards sometimes put out cards which we call specials. These are cards that are included in the regular series but feature unusual or interesting facts about the players. For example, some cards have shown childhood pictures of ball players, others have featured brothers or fathers and sons who are big-league ball players. Some of the specials have included players who have been traded to other teams and players who have set records for their playing performances.

Joe Torre, Boyhood Photo
Topps Company

Lee May and Carlos May
Big League Brothers, Topps Company

Joe Coleman and Joe Coleman, Jr.
Father and Son, Topps Company

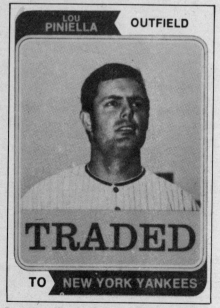

Lou Piniella, Traded, Topps Company

Nolan Ryan, Pitcher
1977 Record Pitcher, Topps Company

It is easy to collect these specials, because only a limited number are printed every year. They are issued in the regular series, and by comparing with other collectors you can find out how many there are in the series. They are also mentioned in the checklists.

Autographs

A very personal and satisfying collection is an autograph collection of sports cards. These are cards which have been signed by the players.

Jon Matlack, Pitcher, Topps Company
An autographed card.

There are a number of ways to get autographed cards. One way is to write to the player asking for his autograph. Enclose the card you want signed and mail it to him in care of his team. If you are lucky the player might put a message on the card along with his autograph. You should put a self-addressed stamped envelope in your letter.

Another way to have your cards autographed is to try to meet the players. When you go to a game, take cards of the players with you. Try to get there early while the players are warming up. Stay near the playing field and ask the players to sign your cards. If you happen to live in an area where a team trains before the regular season, ask someone to take you to the training camp. The players are more available to you there and are generally most happy to autograph your cards.

Clips and Errors
Sometimes sports cards are printed with mistakes on them. The most common mistake in printing is what we call a clip.

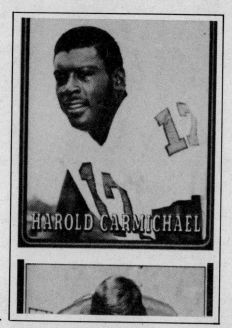

Harold Carmichael and Bruce Jarvis
Topps Company. An example of a clip.

A clip is a card which has parts of two different cards on one card. It looks as if the machine had slipped and didn't print exactly on the card. These clips are easy to spot and fun to have as a special collection.

Errors are cards which have mistakes on them. There are many different kinds of errors. One kind of error is when the player's name is misspelled. Another kind is when the front and

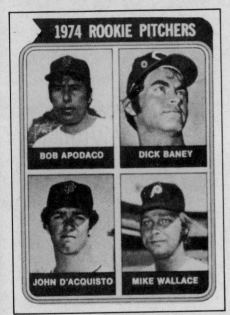

Bob Apodaca with his name misspelled, Topps Company
An example of an error.

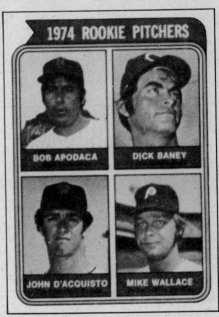

Bob Apodaca, Topps Company

back sides of the card do not match, and the picture of the player on the card is different than the name and information on the back. An example of this is the Topps baseball card issued in 1952 which showed the face of Joe Page on the front but the statistical information of Johnny Sain on the back. An example of a different kind of error is when a batboy was mistaken for a player named Aurelio Rodriguez. A picture was taken of the batboy, and the card was printed with Rodriguez's name and statistics but the picture of the batboy. Another error is the 1959 card of Lou Burdette, a right-handed pitcher, who posed for his card as a left-handed pitcher.

Aurelio Rodriguez card with picture of the Angels' batboy Topps Company

Lou Burdette, Topps Company A right-handed pitcher posing as a left-handed pitcher.

These clips and errors are not common but they can be found. This is an interesting and unusual kind of collection which calls for good detective work on your part.

Other Kinds of Collections

Hall of Fame Cards

Tried and True

A collection of Hall of Fame cards will provide you with cards of the greatest ball players of all time. These cards are not like

HENRY LOUIS GEHRIG
NEW YORK YANKEES · 1923 · 1939
HOLDER OF MORE THAN A SCORE OF
MAJOR AND AMERICAN LEAGUE RECORDS,
INCLUDING THAT OF PLAYING 2130
CONSECUTIVE GAMES. WHEN HE RETIRED
IN 1939, HE HAD A LIFE TIME BATTING
AVERAGE OF 340.

NATIONAL BASEBALL HALL OF FAME & MUSEUM
Cooperstown, New York

u Gehrig, Baseball Hall of Fame Postcard

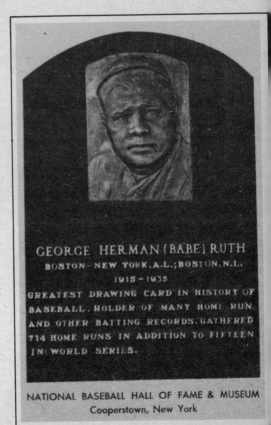

GEORGE HERMAN (BABE) RUTH
BOSTON · NEW YORK, A.L.; BOSTON, N.L.
1915 - 1935
GREATEST DRAWING CARD IN HISTORY OF
BASEBALL. HOLDER OF MANY HOME RUN
AND OTHER BATTING RECORDS. GATHERED
714 HOME RUNS IN ADDITION TO FIFTEEN
IN WORLD SERIES.

NATIONAL BASEBALL HALL OF FAME & MUSEUM
Cooperstown, New York

Babe Ruth, Baseball Hall of Fame Postcard

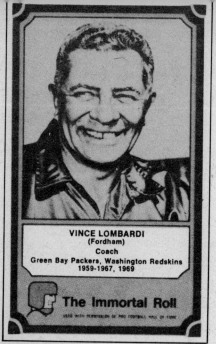

VINCE LOMBARDI
(Fordham)
Coach
Green Bay Packers, Washington Redskins
1959-1967, 1969

The Immortal Roll
USED WITH PERMISSION OF PRO FOOTBALL HALL OF FAME

Vince Lombardi
Football Hall of Fame Card

HAROLD (Red) GRANGE
(Illinois)
Halfback   6-0, 185
Chicago Bears, New York Yankees
1925-1934

The Immortal Roll
USED WITH PERMISSION OF PRO FOOTBALL HALL OF FAME

ARNOLD J. AUERBACH
(1917-   )

ELECTED 1968-COACH

Graduated Eastern District H.S. (Brooklyn) 1935; George Washington U. 1940. Captain and 3-year regular in H.S. and College. Coach at St. Albans Prep and Roosevelt H.S., (D.C.) 1940-43. Joined newly formed NBA in 1946. Led Washington Caps and Tri-Cities to 143 Wins. "Red" took over Boston Celtics in 1950 to lead them to 9 Division Championships and 8 straight World Titles. Coached 11 straight NBA East Teams; won 99 Play-off games. NBA Coach of the Year 1965 en route to 1,037 pro victories. Only coach to win over 1,000 games, leading Boston Celtics to World Professional dominance 1956-66. Washington, D.C. Touchdown Club, Coach of Decade. Wrote outstanding book; traveled internationally for clinics and game promotion. Recipient of several civic awards in career which developed many great players and led Pro Basketball to its greatest recognition and acclaim.

Arnold J. Auerbach
Basketball Hall of Fame Card

Harold "Red" Grange
Football Hall of Fame Card

28

the other sports cards and are different for each sport's Hall of Fame. The cards can be bought either at the Halls of Fame or sent for by mail. Here are the locations of the Halls of Fame:

Baseball Hall of Fame
Cooperstown, New York 13326

Pro Football Hall of Fame
2121 Harrison Avenue N.W.
Canton, Ohio 44708

Naismith Memorial Basketball Hall of Fame
Box 175 Highland Station
460 Alden Street
Springfield, Massachusetts 01109

Minor League Cards   *Up and Coming*

Many minor league teams in the country print sports cards. If you live or travel in an area that has a minor league team

Mike Barlow, Pitcher
Salt Lake Gulls. Minor League Card.

you might find it easy to have the cards autographed. If you want a collection of minor league cards, you can ask for them by writing to the teams. These cards are also advertised for sale in the sports card collectors' magazines. If you would like to know the names and addresses of minor league teams, write to:

National Association of Professional Baseball Leagues
Post Office Box A
St. Petersburg, Florida 33731

Foreign Cards   *Globe Trotter*

The United States is not the only country where sports cards can be found. They are also printed in Europe, Canada, and Japan. In Europe, the most popular cards are basketball and soccer; in Canada, hockey and baseball; and in Japan, baseball. These are difficult to collect, but you can ask people who travel

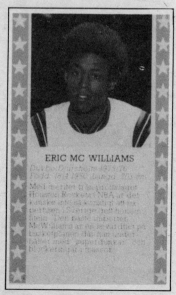

Eric McWilliams
Swedish Basketball Card

Peter Osgood, Southhampton
English Soccer Card

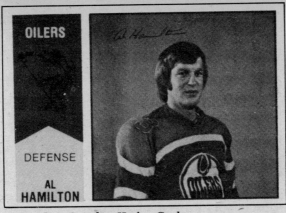

Al Hamilton, Canadian Hockey Card

to bring them back for you. If you have friends in other countries, write to them and ask them to send sports cards from their country.

Premiums   *Eaters*

These are cards that are free with the purchase of certain grocery items like cereals breads, and cupcakes. If you buy the foods that feature these cards you can easily have an eater's

Bill North, Kellogg
3-D Baseball Card
Reprinted with the
permission of Kellogg Company

Forrest Blue, Wonderbread Card
ITT Continental Baking Company, LCA

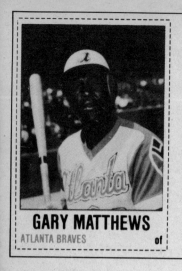

GARY MATTHEWS
ATLANTA BRAVES   of

ERIC SODERHOLM
CHICAGO WHITE SOX   3b

BUMP WILLS
TEXAS RANGERS   2b

Gary Matthews, Eric Soderholm, Bump Wills
Hostess Cupcake Panel
ITT Continental Baking Company, LCA

collection of premium cards. National and regional companies
feature these cards from time to time. The best way for you to
collect these cards is to look for them in the groceries your
family buys or to watch for them at some of the various restau-
rant chains that also feature them.

Superstars   *Big Shots*

A collection of superstars would include the cards of players
who are thought to be the best players in their sport. Because
the cards of players who are superstars can become more valuable in time, this is a collection that can be worth something.
It is sometimes difficult to know what players will be con-
sidered exceptional over a period of years. As time goes by,
you will have fun seeing which players were truly superstars
and which ones were not.

Nolan Ryan, Pitcher
Topps Company

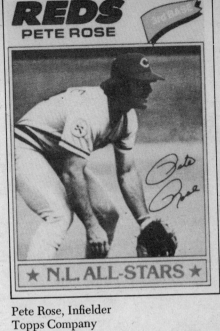

Pete Rose, Infielder
Topps Company

Jim Rice, Outfielder
Topps Company

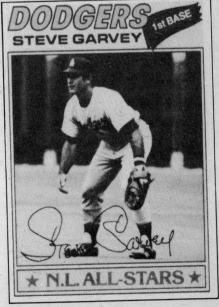

Steve Garvey, First Baseman
Topps Company

TIPS ON HOW TO KEEP A COLLECTION

Now that you are collecting sports cards and they are piling up in your room you should learn how to keep, preserve, and store them.

First sort them into separate piles: one for collecting, one for trading, and one for extras. The extras can be used for playing or making things, so don't throw them away.

The cards that are part of your collection should get special attention. You should keep them in a spot that is easy to get to, like a drawer, shelf, or closet. It's important that the area where you keep them is clean. Be sure to keep them away from windows and out of the kitchen where they can be stained and damaged. Keep your cards orderly and neat so that it will be easy for you to work with them. Here are some of the ways you can store your cards.

Albums

A good way to keep special or favorite cards is in an album. The cards are easy to see and well protected in the album. It is important to remember that you must never glue or tape the cards directly to the album.

These are the different types of albums:

1. *Scrapbook:* You will need a scrapbook and a package of self-sticking "corners." Place a card inside four corners. Wet the four corners and press into the scrapbook.

2. *Loose-leaf Album:* You will need clean sheets of plastic, with pockets, and a hardcover photo album. Put the cards in the pockets and into the album. These items are easy to find; just be sure you can fit your cards into the plastic pockets.

There are albums that are specially designed for sports cards. You can find out where to order these and other materials in collectors' magazines.

Boxes

You will need an empty cigar or shoe box, cellophane tape, felt-tipped pen, and an extra sports card.

Label the box with a description of the collection, and tape the sample card to the outside of the box. Put your cards in order and place them in the box.

Tied

You will need rubber bands, an index card (3″ by 5″), and a pen or pencil.

Write a description of the collection on the index card. Put the index card on top of the pile. Tie with a rubber band. Be sure you don't damage the cards by tying too tightly.

3

How to Read a Sports Card

Each card that you collect will provide you with interesting facts about the player. His name, position, and team are printed on the face of the card. His height, weight, and date and place of birth are on the back, along with a short description of outstanding or unusual things he's done. The career record of the player is also on the back of the card. Many of these statistics are written in abbreviations. Because they can be difficult to understand, we have given you a list of the meanings of the abbreviations. This will help you understand more about the cards.

Baseball	Most Players
AL	American League
NL	National League
G	Games
AB	At Bats
RBI	Runs Batted In
HR	Home Runs
3B	Triples
2B	Doubles
H	Hits
R	Runs
AVG	Batting Average

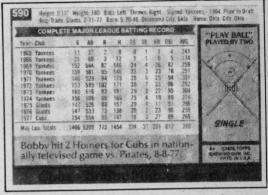

Baseball Player, Topps Company

Baseball Pitcher, Topps Company

Baseball	Pitchers
G	Games Pitched
IP	Innings Pitched
W	Wins
L	Losses
PCT	Percentage of Games Won and Lost
R	Runs
ER	Earned Runs
SO	Strike Outs
BB	Bases on Balls (Walks)
ERA	Earned Run Average

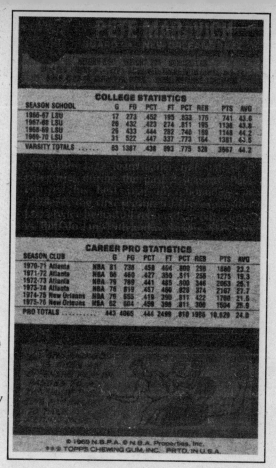

COLLEGE STATISTICS

SEASON SCHOOL	G	FG	PCT	FT	PCT	REB	PTS	AVG
1966-67 LSU	17	273	.452	195	.833	175	741	43.6
1967-68 LSU	26	432	.423	274	.811	195	1138	43.8
1968-69 LSU	26	433	.444	282	.746	189	1148	44.2
1969-70 LSU	31	522	.447	337	.773	164	1381	43.5
VARSITY TOTALS	83	1387	.438	893	.775	528	3667	44.2

CAREER PRO STATISTICS

SEASON CLUB		G	FG	PCT	FT	PCT	REB	PTS	AVG
1970-71 Atlanta	NBA	81	738	.458	404	.800	298	1880	23.2
1971-72 Atlanta	NBA	66	460	.427	355	.811	256	1275	19.3
1972-73 Atlanta	NBA	79	789	.441	485	.800	346	2063	26.1
1973-74 Atlanta	NBA	76	819	.457	469	.826	374	2107	27.7
1974-75 New Orleans	NBA	79	655	.419	390	.811	422	1700	21.5
1975-76 New Orleans	NBA	62	604	.459	396	.811	300	1604	25.9
PRO TOTALS		443	4065	.444	2499	.810	1996	10,629	24.0

© 1969 N.B.P.A. © N.B.A. Properties, Inc.
© TOPPS CHEWING GUM, INC.   PRTD. IN U.S.A.

Basketball Player, Topps Company

Basketball

NBA	National Basketball Association
ABA	American Basketball Association
G	Games
FG	Field Goals (Baskets)
FT	Free Throws
REB	Rebounds
PTS	Total Points—Free throws and field goals combined
AVG	Average of points scored in a game
PCT	Percentages

Hockey	Players
NHL	National Hockey League
WHL	World Hockey League
G	Goals (scored)
A	Assists
P	Total Points
PM	Penalty Minutes

Hockey Player, Topps Company

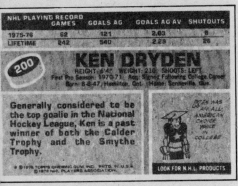

Iockey Goalie, Topps Company

Hockey	Goalie
Goals	Total goals given up in a year
Points	Average of goals given up in a game
Goals AG	Goals scored against the goalie
Goals AG AV	Average of goals scored against the goalie

Football	Quarterback or Running Back
NFC	National Football Conference
AFC	American Football Conference
ATTS	Attempts (to carry, pass, or catch the ball)
YDS	Yards (gained)
AVG	Average number of yards per carry
TDS	Touchdowns
COMP	Completions

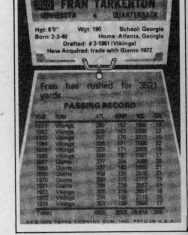

Football Quarterback
Topps Company

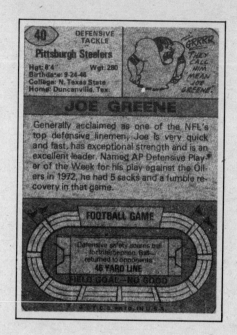

Football Defensive Lineman
Topps Company

ALSO HELPFUL TO KNOW

1. In football the offensive and defensive linemen do not have statistics because they do not carry, pass, or catch the ball.

2. The number in a circle that is printed on the back of the cards is the serial number given to the player by the company that makes the cards. Numbers ending in 0 are reserved for special players.

3. If the year of the card is not printed on the card, you can find out what year it was made by looking at the last year in the career record. The cards have the most recent information about the player for the year before they are issued. For example, if the last year of statistics on the card is 1978, you know that the card was printed the following year, 1979.

☆**4**☆

What Makes Sports Cards Valuable

Many people think of sports cards as clutter or kid stuff and are eager to have them thrown away. They would be very surprised to know how valuable some sports cards are. There is one baseball card alone that is worth over $3,000! And there are serious card-collectors who earn over $20,000 a year selling cards.

You shouldn't expect to become rich collecting sports cards, but you should know that your cards can be worth something. Here are some of the reasons why sports cards are valuable and some of the ways that you can increase the worth of your cards.

AGE

New cards are worth about a penny apiece. Once those cards are ten years old they may be worth a nickel apiece. Very old cards may be worth much more. The longer you keep your cards the more valuable they can become. One reason why old cards are more valuable is that they are reminders of the past;

Eddie Plank Card, 1910

The rare and valuable Honus
Wagner Card. 1907, Sweet Caporal

people enjoy looking at old cards and feeling nostalgic. Another reason why older cards are valuable is that there are fewer of them than new ones.

SCARCITY

Cards are more valuable when they are scarce or in short supply. Most cards today are printed and sold in such large amounts that they are rarely scarce. But cards can become scarce if something unusual happens to them. One example of this is the Eddie Plank card which was issued in 1910. While this card was being printed, the printer's plate broke. A few of the cards had already been printed before it broke, and they are both scarce and valuable today.

The Honus T. Wagner card, issued in 1907, is one of the rarest cards. Mr. Wagner objected to smoking and forced the tobacco company to withdraw his card from the series. The few cards that survived and can be found today are worth over $3,000.

A recent example of scarcity is the story of the "Washington National League" baseball cards. In 1974 it was rumored that the San Diego Padres baseball team was going to be sold and moved to Washington, D. C. Some cards of the Padres players were printed listing them as members of the Washington National League team. The team was not sold and stayed in San Diego. Those Washington National League cards are worth more than the other cards issued in the 1974 series.

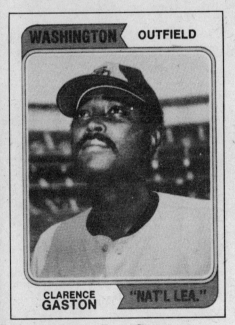

Clarence Gaston, Topps Company
Shown as Washington National
League player.

Clarence Gaston, Topps Company
Shown as San Diego Padres player.

PLAYER

The cards of players who are superstars are worth more than other cards. If you collect these they will become more valuable as time goes by.

SERIES

Sports cards become more valuable when they are gathered into a complete series. If you are a new collector you will find that this is one of the easiest ways to start a valuable collection. If you choose to collect a complete series, keep the cards in numerical order.

CONDITION

Even if your cards are old or scarce, they must be kept in good condition to have value. When cards are new they are in mint condition. The important thing is to try to keep them in this condition. If they are bent, creased, torn, or stained, they lose their value.

Collectors rate the condition of cards in the following ways: MINT—condition is just as when first printed and distributed; the card has no creases or marks; edges not bent; no wear and tear at all on card.
EXCELLENT—slightly worn; shows beginning of wear on edges of card.
VERY GOOD—may be slightly creased; some wear on edges of card.
GOOD (Fair)—card has been roughly handled and shows wear; may be creased and have worn edges.
POOR—just as it says: shows bad condition; creases; marks on card; edges turned back or crumpled.

☆**5**☆

All-Star Albums

The Sporting News All-Time All-Stars team was selected in 1969 to celebrate the one hundred year anniversary of baseball. Members of the Baseball Writers Association of America were asked to vote for a team of the greatest baseball players of all time. The list they voted on was gathered by the fans in each major league city. The fans selected an all-star team for that city and the sportswriters took over from there. These are the players that they chose.

Seven years later, Topps Chewing Gum Company further honored the same ten players by featuring them in their 1976 baseball card series. These all-time all-star cards were numbered 341-350.

The authors have made their own choice of a current all-star team. It was not easy to choose among so many great baseball players. However, they selected who they thought were the best players in their positions at that time.

The Sporting News

LOU GEHRIG
1B

The Sporting News

WALTER JOHNSON
RHP

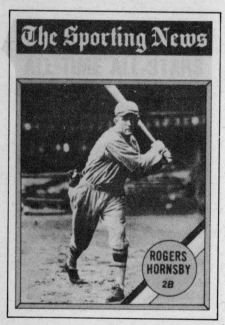

The Sporting News

ROGERS HORNSBY
2B

The Sporting News

TED WILLIAMS
OF

Sporting News All-Time All-Stars, C. C. Johnson Spink, Publisher, The Sporting News

JOHNNY BENCH

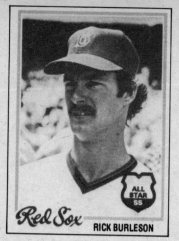

RICK BURLESON

GEORGE FOSTER

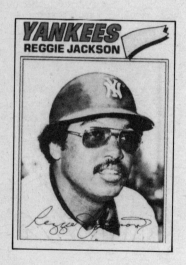

JOE MORGAN

Authors' Choice Current All-Stars

DAVE PARKER

PETE ROSE

TOM SEAVER

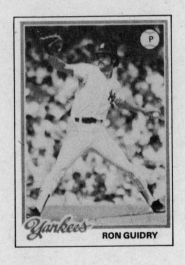

RON GUIDRY

GARRY TEMPLETON

How to Learn More about Sports Cards

WHERE TO GO

The largest collection of sports cards can be found in *The Metropolitan Museum of Art* in New York City. It is called the Burdick Collection and has 350,000 cards. Included are examples of all of the sports cards that have ever been printed. Because this is such an important collection, you must make an appointment to see it. Children under the age of 12 must have an adult with them.

The New York City Public Library also has a collection of cards in its main branch at Forty-second Street and Fifth Avenue. In Room 315 you can see the Goulston Collection of tobacco cards. There are cards dating all the way back to 1887. You must have an adult with you in order to view this collection.

The Football Hall of Fame in Canton, Ohio has interesting displays of the history of football. In addition, you can see their collection of Hall of Fame sports cards.

The Basketball Hall of Fame has a special tribute for their

A sampling of cards from THE METROPOLITAN MUSEUM OF ART
The Jefferson R. Burdick Collection, New York City

A sampling of cards from THE METROPOLITAN MUSEUM OF ART
The Jefferson R. Burdick Collection, New York City

Uniform exhibit in the Pro Football Hall of Fame, Canton, Ohio

"Honor Court" in the Basketball Hall of Fame,
Springfield, Massachusetts

The Baseball Hall of Fame, Cooperstown, New York

members, called an Honor Court. You can see this display and their Hall of Fame cards by visiting them in Springfield, Massachusetts.

The oldest sports hall of fame is *The Baseball Hall of Fame* in Cooperstown, New York. They feature, among other things, a revolving display of baseball cards. Here too you can see their collection of Hall of Fame cards.

A *sports card collectors' convention* is a good place to learn more about cards. People from all over the country come to these conventions to exhibit and sell their cards. You can find out where these shows take place in sports card collectors' magazines or local newspapers.

The revolving display of Baseball Cards
at the Baseball Hall of Fame, Cooperstown, New York

Kids selling their cards at sports card show.

There are *sports card collectors' clubs* that you can join to learn more about cards. These clubs have been formed so that collectors can meet to show, buy, sell, and trade their cards. You can find out about these clubs in your sports card collectors' magazines or at conventions.

WHAT TO READ
Books

There are various books that can be very helpful to you as a sports card collector. One of them is *The Sports Collectors Bible,* which lists all of the cards from the 1880s to the present. Some of the information you will learn includes the company that issued the card and the year it was printed. You will also learn the value of your cards and the number of cards in a particular series. You may obtain this book by writing to:

The Sports Collectors Bible
Wallace-Homestead Book Company
Box B1
Des Moines, Iowa 50304

You might also buy *The Sports Collectors Bible* at collectors' conventions and shows.

Another valuable book that can be purchased at conventions or through hobby magazines is *Sport Americana.* This book lists every card issued in each series from 1934 on. This is an excellent guide for finding out which cards complete your series.

Magazines

There are several good collectors' magazines which you can subscribe to for a moderate price. You will find many interesting articles concerning the history of the hobby and present-day collecting trends. You can learn where and when conventions are held and where local hobby clubs are meeting. There are advertisements for cards for sale or trade as well as cards that are wanted by collectors. By reading these magazines you can get a good idea of what your cards are worth. You can also sell or buy cards by advertising in these magazines. Here is a list of some of these magazines:

The Trader Speaks
3 Pleasant Drive
Lake Ronkonkoma
New York 11779

The Baseball Advertiser
P. O. Box 2
Amawalk, New York 10501

The Sports Collectors Digest
409 North Street
Milan, Michigan 48160

The Collectibles Monthly
P. O. Box 2023
York, Pennsylvania 17405

☆**7**☆

Games to Play with Sports Cards

For as long as kids have been collecting sports cards, they've been playing games with them. These games have been passed along from generation to generation. Some are known by different names in different parts of the country. Some have been played in some areas and not in others. Your parents and grandparents will probably remember a few of these games. If they don't remember these, they might know others they can teach you.

You can play most of the games in this book with friends, but there are a few, like Covers, that you can play by yourself. Just remember to consider which cards you will play with. The cards can be bent, torn, or lost to other players during the game.

These games are for your enjoyment. After you have played some of them you will understand why so many Americans played sports card games when they were young.

COLORS

Object of the Game: The names of the teams are printed in different colors on the face of the card. The object of this game is to match cards by these colors.

Where to Play: Table, floor, or any smooth surface.

Number of Players: 2

Number of Cards: 10 or more per player

How to Play:

1. Each player holds a stack of cards, pictures facing down.
2. The first player takes a card from the top of the stack and places it face up on the table.
3. The second player does the same, placing his or her card on top of the first card.
4. Play continues. The first player whose card's *colors* match the card on the top of the pile, wins the pile.

AGAINST THE WALL

Object of the Game: In this game the players try to knock down cards that are leaning against the wall. They do this by tossing their cards against the standing cards.

Where to Play: Against the side of any wall, indoors or outside.

Number of Players: 2, 3, or 4

Number of Cards: 10 per player

How to Play:

1. Each player leans one card against the wall in an upright position. The cards should be in a row next to each other, about 5 inches apart.

2. All the players stand back about 4 feet from the wall.
3. Each player, in turn, takes a card from his or her own stack of cards and tosses it at the cards leaning against the wall.
4. The player that knocks down the *last* standing card wins all the cards that have been thrown.

DOUBLES

Object of the Game: In this game the players must match the names of the teams, but each player must do it twice before winning a card. This game may be made more difficult by playing it as "triples," when the player must win three times.

Where to Play: Table, floor, or any smooth surface.

Number of Players: 2

Number of Cards: 25 per player

How to Play:

1. Each player holds a stack of cards, pictures facing down.
2. The first player takes a card from the top of his or her stack and places it face up on the table.
3. The second player does the same, placing a card on top of the first card.
4. After a player has matched the *team* of the top card on the pile, the game continues.
5. After a player has matched cards a second time, he or she wins the pile.

STATISTICS

Object of the Game: In this game the winner is the one who has the card with the highest or lowest number in a given statistic.

Where to Play: Table, floor, or any smooth surface.

Number of Players: 2 or more

Number of Cards: 10 or more per player. All of the cards must be of the same sport, with the same statistics; for example, all baseball pitchers.

How to Play:
1. Each player holds cards face up.
2. The first player names the game, states the statistic and whether the number should be highest or lowest. For example, with baseball pitchers one might say "ERA, lowest."
3. Each player turns the top card over on the table. The player whose card has the highest or lowest statistic wins all the cards.
4. Play continues, but the next time the second player names the game.

COVERS or OFF THE WALL

Object of the Game: In this game the player tries to touch or cover one card with another. The player must stand and hold a card flat against the wall. He or she drops it quickly, trying to make it land on any of the cards on the floor.

Where to Play: Against the side of any wall, indoors or outdoors.

Number of Players: 2, 3, or 4
Number of Cards: 10 per player
How to Play:

1. The first player places a card against the wall and lets it drop to the floor.
2. The second player does the same thing.
3. This continues with each player taking turns, until one player manages to have a card land on, or touch, any card lying on the floor. That player then wins all the cards on the floor.
4. Play begins again.

BASEBALL

Object of the Game: In this game the players play baseball with their cards. The player with the most runs after nine innings wins.
Where to Play: Table, floor, or any smooth surface.
Number of Players: 2
Number of Cards: 9 per player. Each player must have a card for each position. For example, you will need 1 pitcher, 1 catcher, 1 first baseman, etc.
How to Play:

1. One player lays his or her cards on the table in the same positions as in a game of baseball. The pitcher is in the center; the three basemen, shortstop, and catcher are placed around him so that the cards form a diamond shape. The three fielders are placed behind the basemen.

2. The other player is "up to bat." He or she holds a card over home plate. The card should be held between the thumb and a finger. The thumb should be at the bottom of the card and the finger should be at the top of the card. Bring thumb and finger together, making the card bend. Then quickly let go so that the card snaps forward.

3. If the card lands on or touches any of the cards on the field, player is out. If the card lands in a free space, player moves the card to first base. If the card lands beyond the outfielders, it is a home run. There are no strikes in this game.

4. Play continues. After three outs, the next player is up. The player who was at bat must now put his or her cards in field position.

5. After nine innings, the player with the most runs wins the game and all of the cards.

WAR

Object of the Game: On the printed side of the card, you will find a number inside of a circle. It is usually in one corner of the card. In this game, the highest number wins.

Where to Play: Table, floor, or any smooth surface.

Number of Players: 2

Number of Cards: 26 per player

How to Play:

1. Each player holds cards with the pictures facing up.

2. Each player takes a card from the top of his or her

stack and places it on the table with the printed side facing up.

3. The player whose card has the highest number wins, and takes both cards.

4. If the players put down cards with the same number, it is war. They both must put down three more cards. The player whose *third* card has the highest number, wins the pile.

5. The game continues until one player has no cards left.

HEADS AND TAILS or MATCHING

Object of the Game: In this game, the picture side of the card is heads. The printed side of the card is tails. The players must match heads and tails to win.

Where to Play: Table, floor, or any smooth surface.

Number of Players: 2

Number of Cards: 10 or more per player

How to Play:

1. The first player flips three cards in the air. The ones that land with the picture showing are heads. The ones that land with the printed side showing are tails.

2. The second player flips three cards in the air, trying to match the first player's heads and tails. For example, if the first player flips two heads and a tail, the second player must flip two heads and a tail to get a match. If it is a match, the second player wins the cards. If it is not a match, the first player wins the cards.

3. The game continues, but the second player now flips first.

GOTTAS

Object of the Game: In this game the players must match the names of the teams. For example, a Yankee matches a Yankee. It takes *three matching team cards in a row* to win.

Where to Play: Table, floor, or any smooth surface.

Number of Players: 2

Number of Cards: 25 or more per player

How to Play:

1. Each player holds cards with the pictures facing down.
2. The first player takes a card from the top of his or her stack and places it on the table face up.
3. The second player does the same, placing a card on top of the first card.
4. Play continues. The first player to place the *third* matching team card in a row, wins the pile.

POSITIONS

Object of the Game: In this game the players must match the playing position of the players. For example, a catcher matches a catcher.

Where to Play: Table, floor, or any smooth surface.

Number of Players: 2

Number of Cards: 10 or more per player

How to Play:

1. Each player holds cards with the pictures facing down.
2. The first player takes a card from the top of his or her stack and places it on the table face up.
3. The second player does the same, placing a card on top of the first card.
4. The first player to place a card on the pile that matches the *position* of the top card, wins the pile.

Making Things with Sports Cards

When extra cards pile up, don't throw them away! Gather them up and put them to good use. There are many ways to use sports cards that you may not have thought of.

To give your bicycle a snappy sound, try clipping a sports card to the frame of your bike. Use a clothespin to hold it and be sure the card is touching the spokes. As you pedal your bike, the card will "snap" against the spokes of the bike.

Or, when your baseball hat begins to lose its shape, put a card inside the cap, above the front brim. This will stiffen the peak of the cap.

In this chapter you will find nine more ways to use your extra cards. These projects are easy to make and can be made from things you already have in your home.

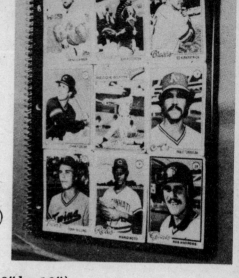

☆ Notebook

What You Need

Spiral or loose-leaf notebook
   (8½" by 12" is standard size)
24 sports cards
Glue
2 sheets of self-sealing plastic (10" by 12")

What You Do

1. Arrange the cards face up on the front of the notebook, three across and three down. This will cover the notebook and leave a small margin all around.
2. One at a time, glue the back of each card and press it in place, face up, on the notebook.
3. Turn the notebook over and follow the same procedure on the back cover.
4. Place a heavy book over the notebook and allow to dry.
5. Take the plastic sheets and carefully cover the front and the back of the notebook. It is easiest if you start at the top and slowly work down to the bottom of the notebook.

You now have your own special notebook for school with a covering that will protect it from the rain.

☆ Homework Pad

What You Need
A small notepad (about 3½″ by 4″)
Dark-colored, felt-tipped pen
Sports card
Glue
Self-sealing plastic sheet (4″ by 4½″)

What You Do
1. With the felt-tipped pen, color a 1″ border around the front cover of the notepad.
2. Spread a thin layer of glue on the back of the card.
3. Press the card, face up, on the center of the notepad.
4. Put a heavy book on top of the pad until the glue has dried.
5. Carefully cover the front of the pad with the clear plastic.

☆ Baseball-Card Holder

What You Need
Styrofoam ball (baseball size)
Black, felt-tipped pen
Dull knife
2 baseball sports cards
Jar lid (about 2½″ diameter)

What You Do
1. Use the black pen to draw stitches, like those on a baseball, on the styrofoam ball.
2. With the knife, make slits in the styrofoam large enough to slide the cards in. Insert cards.
3. Turn the jar lid upside down and rest the ball in it.

You can keep this in your room as a decoration or make enough of them to give as favors at a party.

☆ Room Decoration

What You Need
Paper hole puncher
9 sports cards
String or cord (42″ long)
2 thumbtacks

What You Do
1. Punch a hole in the top corners of each of the cards. Every card will have two holes. Punch the holes at least ¼″ in from the edge.
2. Pull the string through the holes of all nine cards. The face of each card should face front. Space the cards evenly along the string. Leave about 6″ of the string at each end.
3. Tack this up in your room. This will fit across a window that measures 32″ in width. Or you might want to tack it to the wall.

You can make this longer or shorter if you like. You can change the cards at any time. You might want to hang baseball cards in the summer, football cards in the fall, etc.

☆ Sports Picture Collage

What You Need

Sports cards; newspaper or magazine clippings
Piece of cardboard the size you want your collage to be
Glue
Scissors
Yarn or string

What You Do

1. Select sports cards, newspaper headlines, or pictures, and arrange them on the cardboard. These can overlap one another.
2. When you have an arrangement that you like, spread a thin layer of glue on the back of the cards and pictures and then put them on the cardboard. Let picture dry.
3. Make two holes at the top of your picture, run the string through them, and tie. Your collage is ready to be hung.

You should use a theme for your collage. For example, you might make one of your favorite player or team or sport. This makes a nice gift for a friend.

☆ Pen and Pencil Holder

What You Need
1 empty milk carton (quart size)
Ruler and pencil
Scissors
Colored paper
Glue
4 sports cards

What You Do
1. With the pencil and ruler, measure and mark off 4½" from the bottom of the carton. Do this all around the carton.
2. Cut off the top part.
3. Measure and cut a piece of colored paper (about 4½" by 12").
4. Spread a thin layer of glue on the paper and carefully wrap it around the carton. Let it dry.
5. Spread a thin layer of glue on the back of four sports cards.
6. Carefully glue them to the four sides of the carton. Let them dry. To prevent the edges of the cards from curling, put rubber bands around the top, middle, and bottom of the box until the cards are dry.

☆ Desk Pad

What You Need
15 sports cards
Cardboard (15″ by 13″)
Colored mystic tape, or colored cloth tape
Sheets of self-sealing plastic (clear)

What You Do
1. Lay the cards out on the cardboard, five across and three down. There will be a 1″ margin all around the cardboard.
2. One at a time glue the back of each card and press it, face up, in place on the cardboard.
3. Cover the border on all four sides with the colored tape.
4. With the plastic sheets, carefully cover the entire desk pad, including the border. This will make the pad last longer and give it an even writing surface.

☆ Party Invitations

What You Need

A package of small notecards and envelopes (about 3″ by 4″)
   (If you can't buy plain ones you can use the ones with writing on them, like thank-you notes. Just be sure the inside of the card is blank.)
Sports cards, one for each invitation
Glue

What You Do

1. Spread a thin layer of glue on the back of the sports card. Press the sports card, face up, on the center of the notecard. Continue until all of your invitations have a sports card glued to the front.
2. Allow the glue to dry. If you place a heavy book on the cards, the ends will not curl up.
3. Write your message, or invitation, on the inside of the notecard.

☆ Personalized Baseball Card

What You Need

A photograph of yourself in uniform, or a photograph of your
    face with your baseball cap on (approximately 2″ by 3″)
1 baseball card—a card of your favorite team
Scissors
Glue
Colored adhesive tape

What You Do

1. Cut your photograph neatly so that it fits within the border of the baseball card. The name of the team should show.
2. Glue the photograph to the baseball card.
3. Cut thin strips of tape and make a new border around the photograph. Make sure that the name of the team still shows.

Index

About the Authors

MARGO MCLOONE, born and raised in Waseca, Minnesota, played and traded sports cards with her seven brothers and sisters when she was small. Today, she makes her home in New York City, where she is a junior high school English teacher. The co-author of *The Herb and Spice Book for Kids*, she holds a BA from Clarke College, Dubuque, Iowa, and an MA from the New School for Social Research, New York City.

ALICE SIEGEL, co-author of *The Herb and Spice Book for Kids*, lives in Scarsdale, New York, with her husband and three sons—all avid sports cards collectors. She became interested in this great hobby as a result of their interest. With a BS degree from New York University and an MA from Manhattan College, she is presently a reading consultant for a suburban school district.